SUMMARY OF

HOAX

DONALD TRUMP, FOX NEWS, AND THE
DANGEROUS DISTORTION OF TRUTH

BY BRIAN STELTER

Proudly Brought To You By
OneHour Reads

D1366353

Table of Contents

EXECUTIVE SUMMARY

In a world that is so easily beset with lies, hypocrisy and any other ploy you can think of, Brian Stelter, with this book, is attempting a gradual rewrite of the narrative. Titled *Hoax: Donald Trump, Fox News and the Dangerous Distortion of Truth*, Stelter draws on three years of interviews with over 140 staffers at Fox, 180 former staffers and other knowledgeable sources. Assuming a citizen's position, Stelter advocates for factual journalism, exposing all the ills that the President of the United States and the Fox News media have wrought.

If you have ever been interested in knowing what happens on the American media scene- the truth of what really goes down, then, this is a must-read for you. An exciting eye-opener it is! Happy reading!

PROLOGUE

KEY TAKEAWAYS

- By the 26th day of March, 2020, the fast spreading coronavirus had raked a thousand deaths in the United States.
- Whenever the *Times* newspaper published a critique of the Trump administration, which were always true, Trump would claim that the *Times* was fake, and failing.
- Rich people like Hannity had managed to downplay the virus, looking just as ignorant as the president.
- Trump needed Fox, relying solely on propagandists like Hannity to fill him with whatever it is he wanted to hear.

As at the 26th of March, 2020, what the people of the United States needed desperately was a leader. Unfortunately for them, they didn't get that. Rather, they were slammed with Sean Hannity and the current president of the United States- Donald Trump.

The round number, one thousand had become a dreaded one. It was the same number that began the 26th day of March, 2020. The fast spreading coronavirus had raked a thousand deaths in the United States. With six minutes apart from the next, an American died from the disease. Worse still, most Americans knew that the figures were higher than what was being disclosed, considering that several people died in their homes without even getting tested. By the end of the day, the number of deaths had reached one thousand, one hundred and ninety-five.

The worst hit was Trump's own hometown in New York- Queens. The Elmhurst Hospital Center was located there. Several sick persons lined up in the cold weather, praying for the chance to see a doctor. Like most hospitals, Elmhurst had exhausted its beds, after which ventilators would follow suit. The hospital hallways were crowded with patients too sick to even say their own names.

The scene was terrible, and very far from the hopeful image which the White House must have created in the minds of many. As a result, two young doctors put their jobs on the line in a bid to let the public in on the true state of things. The doctors, known as Dr. Colleen Smith and Dr. Ashley Bray, through their efforts helped the public understand the severity of the situation. Smith made a video recording of the hospital's insides on her phone and sent it to *The New York Times*. Likewise, Dr. Bray informed a reporter with the *Times* about the increasing number of deaths in the hospital. This description put forward by Dr. Bray heralded a turning point in the way the public understood the crisis.

However, President Trump did not read this story. Months before this, he had claimed proudly that he cancelled the subscription the White House made to the *Times*. Whenever the newspaper published a critique of the Trump administration, which was always true, Trump would claim that the *Times* was fake, and failing. So did his friends at Fox News. The twist here is that there were a few true and committed journalists who worked at Fox and knew that their counterparts were only lying. More than anything, they wished that sources like Bray and Smith would reach out to them, rather than reach out to *The New York Times*. However, they also knew that the misbehavior of their peers made it impossible for such to happen. Rich people like Hannity had managed to downplay the virus, looking just as ignorant as the president.

Fox correspondents tried all they could to report the news. On five different shows, they shared Bray's quote. Sadly, viewers like Trump had been trained to disbelieve whatever was said by other news outlets. For some reason, they also did not want to believe it was that bad.

There was a terrible lack of trust, beginning from the top. Truth is, Trump did not trust even the news anchors on Fox News. He told his aides that these news anchors had a tendency to be nasty. He also added that some of them ought to be with CNN or MSNBC, and not with Fox- the network which he promoted to his huge followers. Let's get this straight. Trump did not ramble about Fox because of his niceness, if there were any good ness in him really. Trump needed Fox. He relied solely on propagandists like Hannity to fill him with whatever it is he wanted to hear. If there was anything Trump needed Fox for, it was for the sole purpose of keeping his substitute reality intact.

It is for this reason that Trump was scheduled to call in to Hannity's show at 9pm. That very day, it was as though 9pm wouldn't come soon enough for the President of the United States. The daily press briefing on the Covid-19 virus which had held earlier in the day had been nothing but a total disaster. At 5:30, Trump had gone before the cameras, telling the people to relax. He also publicly revealed his affections for Tom Brady while attacking the news media which he described as corrupt.

After spending thirty-nine minutes which were misleading by the way, Donald Trump left the briefing, went on to order dinner and then waited for his turn on Hannity. The imbalance of power was so visible- The president was blessed with tons of world leaders, joint chiefs and the cabinet. Yet, when it came to an interview on Fox News, Trump was simply another caller who had to be put onto the control room switchboard.

Like always, Hannity began the show with his sermon about Democrats endangering the country. This time around, he dug into the New York governor, Andrew Cuomo, alongside the New York City mayor, Bill de Blasio. Hannity said that by criticizing Trump, both men politicized a national emergency, adding that both Cuomo and Blasio needed to stop. He then went on to politicize the national emergency himself with his caller's help- Donald, from Queens. Queens, really?

For a moment, Hannity freaked out. He had tried to find out if Trump was at the other end of the call. He heard nothing. Shortly after, however, he heard Trump say he was right there. Trump went on as he began by flattering his facilitator, claiming to have postponed an important call with Chinese president, Xi Jinping so as to talk with Hannity. As though that were not enough, Trump went on to say that it simply meant that Hannity had the best rated show on television. This was nothing but a big, fat lie. There were several other shown on television that had swallowed Hannity's show; for instance, NBC Nightly News, American Idol, Wheel of Fortune, etc. Sadly, all Trump was referring to was cable. He wasn't particularly interested in the broadcast networks. Trump was simply a cable guy, and the highlight of his day was his call with Hannity.

This thing isn't one I would describe as an interview, but even if it were, it was a complete love-in and a lie fest. However, there was a tiny streak of truth present in Trump's first answer. He actually kept the Chinese president waiting. He mentioned to Hannity that he would be speaking with the Chinese president by ten-thirty, after their call.

Beijing is no dunce, I guess. They noticed Trump's stunt and decided to keep him waiting for some time after ten-thirty. At around 1:19am, Trump tweeted about having just finished a great conversation with the president of China.

On the political scene, unfortunately, Trump's forty-minute chat with Hannity carried more consequence. The remarks made by Trump were proof that he hadn't really come to terms with the urgency of the pandemic. He went as far as acknowledging that he doubted the computer models which led Cuomo to plead for thirty thousand ventilators, saying that he felt a lot of the numbers being said in some areas were more than they were actually going to be.

In the final analysis, New York did not need as much as thirty thousand ventilators, and this was mainly because front-liners took drastic steps to guard against the spread of the pandemic. In the absence of massive social distancing, tons and tons of ventilators and coffins would have been needed. Unfortunately, the default setting which Trump held was one of disbelief. He just didn't believe. He was very comfortable with disbelief.

A number of Hannity's colleagues tried to express their displeasure at the nonsense going on. A radiologist and medical commentator for Fox news, Dr. Saphier said on air the next day that he was aware of the shortage of ventilators. Network management was at home with this line of action, hoping that guests were able to rebut the president's remarks. More than anything, they wanted to be able to show that Fox was capable of accommodating several, different points of view. However, they also knew that Saphier's comment which aired at 1pm in the afternoon was only viewed by a tiny portion of the audience Hannity had. Noting beat prime time. Unfortunately, management had no control over prime time.

THE CREATION

KEY TAKEAWAYS

- Back then, experts felt that MSNBC would be the channel that would pose the greatest challenge to CNN, not Fox news.
- The number of persons who left forced NBC boss, Bob Wright to place a call across to Ailes, accusing Ailes of poaching his staffers.
- A writer once admitted that Ailes says uncouth, horrible things which make newspaper stories more interesting.
- Through the use an alter ego, Trump lied his way onto the *Forbes* 400 list, as well as defend himself in the pages of *The New York Times*.

Far back as 1996, when Donald Trump made the decision to buy buildings and beauty pageants, Rupert Murdoch decide he was buying Roger Ailes. Murdoch gave a huge sum of money to the GOP political operative for the sole purpose of building him a news channel. This channel was located in the basement of the News Corp building in the legendary city of New York. In modern American history, this was one of the most crucial decisions ever taken.

Ailes did not partner with Murdoch without intentions of his own. Not only did he have personal reasons, he also had political motivations. First off, he desperately wanted the Republican Party to win on television, in the same manner that Rush Limbaugh was taking the lead on radio. He also wanted to make a point to his former bosses at NBC. These bosses of his had taken the channel right out of his hands to create MSNBC.

Back then, experts felt that MSNBC would be the channel that would pose the greatest challenge to CNN, not Fox news. As a matter of fact, Fox was viewed as being least likely to succeed. As for NBC and ABC, they had created news divisions to draw from. At the time, Fox had no news infrastructure in place. Things seemed so bad that Ted Turner had said he was going to squelch Rupert like a bug. However, Murdoch and Ailes turned these jeers into fuel. Rather than become intimidated, they made a vow to make Fox No. 1.

A lot of Ailes's former lieutenants believed in him and left NBC for the new channel. According to Ailes, eight two staffers came to Fox with him, although I was told that they were more like fifty. Regardless of what the actual number was, the number of persons who left forced NBC boss, Bob Wright to place a call across to Ailes, accusing Ailes of poaching his staffers. Ailes responded to this accusation saying that Wright was finding it difficult to differentiate between a recruitment and a jailbreak.

Just like Trump, Ailes viewed himself as a counterpuncher. One thing he usually and proudly told his executives was to avoid picking fights with anyone who liked to fight. In this case, Ailes was fighting against the entire media establishment. His previous boss, Richard Nixon, would have been so proud of him at a time like this. Back in the seventies, Nixon, along with VP Spiro Agnew believed strongly that they were at a war with a liberal cabal of television networks run by elites whom Agnew once described as small and unelected. With time, terms like media bias found a place in the lexicon. It was only a matter of time before the early nineties came on board, and media bias became highly waged against. Hence, when Ailes mentioned that his channel would promote fairness and balance, suggesting that the rest of television news tilted towards the left, millions of conservatives completely understood what he was saying.

In July 1996, Ailes attended the Television Critics Association's press tour. There, he announced the name of his new channel. Prior to his taking the stage, reporters got wind of a handout which revealed poor public opinions of the press. The handout was a fake news manifesto. The handout cited one poll where only 14 percent of respondents gave journalists positive marks and another where 67 percent said TV news was biased. The solution was simply Ailes and Fox. He went as far as swearing that all Fox News wanted to give people were the facts and information. He was in no way oblivious of what he was doing. In fact, he knew exactly what he was doing. He however insisted that he was simply announcing that Fox News would provide unbiased coverage, regardless of whether people were traumatized by it, or not.

Television critics found Ailes irresistible. On a more practical note, he began to write their columns for them. In fact, following the tour appearance, a writer admitted that Ailes says uncouth, horrible things which make newspaper stories more interesting. I'm pretty sure this guy reminds you of someone.

For several decades, Trump and Ailes ran in the same New York media circles. Ailes would proudly say that himself and Trump were really good friends for over twenty-five years. Trump, on the other hand would state that Roger owed him. Both men shared a lot of similarities. They both had the same fears of crime, same racist opinions about immigration and a whole lot more. They were both born within the same generation, with Ailes being only six years older than Trump. They both cheated on their wives and had serious paranoia. Most importantly, both of them ran their businesses in such a way that they dominated the scene, exercising absolute control. If Ailes was the subject, all of Fox hosts knew that they had to rain credit on him whenever he wrote a book or was giving a speech. With Trump, lieutenants had to be reminded that he had a wandering mind whenever the conversation wasn't about him.

The two men largely appreciated public relations and the power it wielded, whether it was in the building up of their brands via puffy magazine profiles or knocking a rival off through a well-placed hit piece. Trump saw no difference between PR and the press. When opportune, Trump used the press to gather more points unto himself, promoting his own interests. Jimmy Breslin, the late communist reported that Trump took over news reporters in New York City through the art of the return phone call. According to Breslin, all it took Trump to control the city's news media was two minutes of making soft, bussing sounds over the phone.

It didn't matter whether Trump was referring to a personal feud or a business scheme, he was a very reliable source of gossip for columnists who had spaces to fill up. All of this coverage was impressive to the bankers with whom Trump was kept afloat. Breslin mentioned that Trump lived by rules set by his dad. These rules ranged from never using your own money, stealing a good idea and claiming it's yours, doing anything at all to get publicity to remembering that everyone could be bought.

Bought, or maybe, conned. When reporters were in dire search of a tantalizing story, they sometimes took dictations from John Barron. In the real sense of things, this John Barron was Donald Trump, pretending as a flack for Donald Trump. Through the use of this alter ego, Trump lied his way onto the *Forbes* 400 list, as well as defend himself in the pages of *The New York Times.* The creation of this alter ego was inspired by Fred Trump, Trump's father. He had used the same tactic in his own business.

The minute Trump had a first-name status in the press, he did away with his disguise, and began dishing tips out to writers who kept him anonymous. In some cases, they'd describe Trump as a source close to Trump. He continued to employ this technique while in the White House, with Hannity being the greatest beneficiary.

Hannity had no reason to get any form of approval from his bosses before citing his sources. Whenever he wanted, he could say anything. On the 2nd of January, 2020, a few minutes before airtime, Trump informed Hannity about the Baghdad airstrike which killed the Iranian General Qassem Soleimani. All this while, Hannity was on vacation. So, he called in to his own show and recited all that Trump told him. All of this information, he claimed he got from sources.

Whatever the president wanted, he pushed for through Hannity. Dutifully, Hannity attributed the information to sources whom he never named, claiming that he had sources and access to special knowledge, constantly deriding the practice of journalism.

Like him, Trump was nothing but a big hypocrite. He repeatedly told Americans to avoid trusting anyone who reported any information anonymously. He claimed that such information was made up by members of the media who then attributed them to sources. Ironically, he was at the time Hannity's greatest anonymous source. On that level, lying had become a pathological thing. Trump however had a good thing going. By his side, he had a world of pro-Trump media operators. There was no need to play John Barron anymore. He already had tons of John Barrons.

THE CANDIDATE

KEY TAKEAWAYS

- History has it that there was a point in time when Rupert Murdoch firmly told Donald Trump to calm down.
- Eventually, Carlson's own tapes became Ailes's undoing.
- Carlson was not the first Fox anchor to gather substantial evidence against Ailes to be used in case of termination.
- A couple of months after the lawsuit landed, several women came out to accuse Trump of misconduct.

It might be difficult to imagine now, but history has it that there was a point in time when Rupert Murdoch firmly told Donald Trump to calm down.

It was the 18th of February, 2016. Gradually, Murdoch was giving in to Trump. He was reluctant about the whole thing and it was visible enough on Twitter. Following the first debate, Trump flared up and lashed out at Kelly. Murdoch's response to the entire thing was to defend Fox's moderation, and claim that Trump had to learn that he was in a public life. On the 15th of December, 2015, Murdoch tweeted that Trump appeared to be getting more thin-skinned, asking if flying around the country was getting Trump tired.

All through the campaign season, the candidate watched Fox in order to get talking points, employed Fox to subjugate his opposition and then returned to complain that Fox was manipulating the coverage. Constantly, he was on the phone with Ailes ranting about sights which he perceived. Murdoch finally got to hear about all these.

Trump not only ranted in private, he did same in public. On the 17th of February, 2016, he claimed that Fox did not want him to win. The following day, he went on to accuse Murdoch of rigging a scientific poll. It was at this time that Rupert spoke to Donald like a grandfather would speak to his toddler grandchild.

Rupert had always wanted a very cordial relationship with the US president. The kind of relationship that would allow him gain access into the oval office whenever he wanted. He wanted to enjoy all the state dinner invites and policy briefings. Trump could be his gateway to all of these if he would only calm down.

Trump continually came up with new ways to attack Kelly. Fox executives were mad a t Trump as they fumed at him. They also fumed at the RNC for failing to corral the guy, as well as the press for taking pleasure in the feud. Honestly? They were not feuding. Trump was simply thrashing about, wildly, in a bid to cull Kelly from the Fox herd and make a scapegoat out of her. Almost every week in the course of the primaries, a Fox executive grumbled about the GOP front-runner. They all said different things. Some said he was nuts, while others described him as being out of control. However, all their complaints didn't do much because when Trump wasn't upset with Fox, and Fox producers weren't cursing over Trump, he was live with Hannity or O'Reilly or Greta Van Susteren or *Fox & Friends or Special Report* or *Fox News Sunday*. All his rallies were carried live by Fox and all cable TV. The

Trump campaign was fought mostly on television, while the rallies became elaborate stages for the show.

Kelly took note of all the interviews, rallies and the live shots. She was hurt, and felt like Ailes did very little to defend her. Others on the inside saw it the same way. On the other hand, Ailes wasn't sure as to what more Kelly wanted from him. Even though many people considered him a powerful force to reckon with in the world of politics, many failed to realize that he was losing it in his final years. There was very little fight left in him. Sadly, his history of abuse was finally catching up with him.

On the 6th of July, 2016, Gretchen Carlson sued Roger Ailes. Trump couldn't believe it. He thought the lawsuit was a hoax. That lawsuit became one that may never be forgotten in history. Carlson was bold in his legal filing. He exposed all of Ailes's predatory tactics, brought Fox news into the issue, disturbed Trump's presidential race, and lastly, birthed the flame that would later become the #MeToo movement. This Ailes's scandal prompted *The New York Times* to look even more deeply into Billy O'Reilly. This line of action led the *Times* reporters to investigate Harvey Weinstein. Now, Weinstein is locked up behind bars, making the world a better place.

There is however a part of the story that very few people know about- this plan dates back several years ago. Carlson's suit accused Steve Doocy, her former co-host of sexual harassment. Somehow, Fox managed to delete this part of her complaint. As far as I know, the claims against Doocy were never thoroughly looked into. However, Carlson made mention that Doocy's misconduct went on for years. As a matter of fact, it was the first thing she mentioned when she called her attorney, Martin Hyman, in 2014.

At the time, Carlson was off *Fox & Friends*. In the year 2013, Ailes took her off the morning show and gave her the 2pm hour. As if this wasn't clear enough that she had been demoted, he went on to slash her pay. She tried to make the most of her new position, booking Trump as her inaugural guest, as she leveraged her a.m. show connection from his weekly phone calls. At some point, Trump tweeted that Gretchen will be a big success. It was, kind of. Carlson held hers, but it was at one of the least rated hours of the day. She began to feel underutilized by the firm, and disrespected by Ailes. Ailes continued to ogle and flirt around her. Another one of Ailes's targets who goes by the name, Alisyn Camerota referred to Ailes's harassment as emotional harassment. Simply put, this was bullying for the purpose of showing who the boss is and keeping everyone in their place. Carlson mentioned that towards the end of Camerota's stay at Fox, she started refusing to go to Roger's office. Carlson continued to go to his office, but began to go along with a tape recorder.

Initially, she consulted with Hyman, telling him about Doocy and the situation of things at Fox. She mentioned being worried that Ailes would do as much as exercise a year out in her three-year contract and just dump her. What she wanted was advice. Hyman told her to be measured in her meetings with Ailes, adding that Ailes might be tape recording her. Carlson was confused. She asked if Ailes could do that. Hyman then went on to explain that certain states, of which New York was inclusive were categorized as one-party consent states. This simply meant that one person was capable of taping without telling anyone else.

Eventually, Carlson's own tapes became Ailes's undoing.

Carlson was not the first Fox anchor to gather substantial evidence against Ailes to be used in case of termination. In this case however, Hyman's co-counsel, Nancy Erika Smith reported that Carlson intended to sue, even if Ailes let her keep her job. By June 2016, Hyman and Smith had drafted a plan for filing the suit in September. They had also started drafting the paperwork. Unfortunately, Ailes decided to end her on the day her contract expired- the 23rd of June. The top lawyer at Fox news, Dianne Brandi, along with Bill Shine called Carlson in and made it known to her that she would not be allowed to return on-air to say goodbye.

Carlson had already scheduled a vacation. Hence, she asked Shine and Brandi for some time to process the news before she would sign her exit papers. They agreed. She left the building and called her legal team, telling them to prepare for battle. The legal filing which was slated for two weeks later completely threw Ailes off balance. He was so disturbed that he couldn't come up with a public response for a whole day. Even privately, he described Carlson as a crazy bitch, adding that her ratings sucked.

Trump was also livid. Not particularly because Ailes had assaulted women for years, but because he felt that Carlson was trying to take a great man down. A couple of months after the lawsuit landed, several women came out to accuse Trump of misconduct. Trump found the event sad, and began thinking up ways to help Roger. He then re-awakened his old, social network.

Most of the men within this network believed in Roger's attack rule. It was on this premise that Ailes built Fox. It was also on this premise that Hannity built his profile. Trump, likewise won the GOP primary on the basis of the attack strategy. All these men were in constant communication with one another. Since the suit was filed by Carlson in New Jersey Superior Court, Trump told Ailes to hire Michael Sirota as his attorney. Oddly, Sirota had helped Trump resolve all of his Atlantic City casino drama. Sirota specialized in bankruptcy and corporate restructuring. Hence, Trump's recommendation made little or no sense. However, Sirota, in a bid to help called in a crisis PR person known as Karen Kessler.

Kessler and her partner, Warren Cooper drove to Ailes's home in Cresskill, New Jersey, where they found him in a rather huge chair, hooked up to an IV stand, with a nurse dispensing whatever it was. In another room of the house, Rudy Giuliani was on the phone. Rudy wanted to steer Fox's internal investigation so that Ailes would be cleared and Carlson would be humiliated. However, Rupert Murdoch's sons wanted this matter to be taken seriously. Both sons had fought with and lost to Ailes before. This was their chance to get even and get control of Fox. Ailes explained this family drama to Trump in one of his calls with the candidate.

Things came to a head during the GOP convention in Cleveland, Ohio. When the convention began on Monday, July 18, Ailes was still convinced he could survive Carlson's attack, as he called it. Hannity still supported him. Guilfoyle still leaned on reluctant colleagues to get on Team Roger, tempting them with promotions she couldn't actually deliver. But Guilfoyle didn't have power anymore and neither did Ailes. Rupert called on Monday morning and urged him to step down. He told Ailes to agree to resign, he said, so that the situation wouldn't get any messier. When the call leaked, the entire Quicken Loans Arena in Cleveland lit up with the news.

THE COMMANDER

KEY TAKEAWAYS

- Regardless of all the talks going around about togetherness and common humanity, it would do us a world of good to understand that there are huge differences between the liberals and the conservatives.
- Over the years, studies have shown significant differences in brain chemistry between liberals and conservatives.
- In the same manner as many of Fox's super fans, Trump resented news outlets that failed to reflect his own view of the world.

On how many occasions have you heard people ask what's wrong in reference to Hannity or Rachel Maddow's fans? The truth remains that whether they're right, or wrong, they are different. Regardless of all the talks going around about togetherness and common humanity, it would do us a world of good to understand that there are huge differences between the liberals and the conservatives. Fox and Trump intensify those differences.

Over the years, studies have shown significant differences in brain chemistry between liberals and conservatives. Some people are naturally wired to value tradition and preservation. These people have more likelihood to perceive threats from outsiders. A study once showed frightening images to participants. These images ranged from maggots in an open wound to a crowd fighting with a man. At the end of the survey, it was discovered that conservatives had stronger reactions to the images than liberals. This pretty much explains Fox's fear-based appeals.

Up until the day of the election in 2016, Fox fans were way more pessimistic about the future of America, critical of Obama's performance and much more scared of Clinton being president, in comparison to the general American public. Fear was a common denominator among them. Night after night, Fox's highest rated show strengthened this point of view. Trump benefitted largely from this.

In October, a survey that was conducted revealed that people who trusted Fox over other networks were gloomier about the health of the economy than people who trusted CNN or CBS. A meagre eleven percent of Fox fans said America was in an economic recovery, a recovery that had been going on for years. More than other consumers, Fox loyalists were more likely to say they were concerned about political fraud, media bias, and the bogey of voter fraud which Trump kept talking about.

Several of these viewers were primed to lose, which made Trump's victory much more shocking. At this point, they felt they were gaining control of power for the first time in several years, in the weirdest ways and with the most surprising set of leaders. Fox appeared to be the home team, as one of the network's major fans became president of the United States. In the same manner as many of Fox's super fans, Trump resented news outlets that failed to reflect his own view of the world. He had now been blessed with the power to do something about that, and was determined to delegitimize anyone who posed as an obstruction to him.

In January 2017, while Trump was still the president-elect, he clinched on the fake news term. The term was coined by researchers and reporters to describe false stories which were simply fabricated on social media. Trump took the term as a punchline. Fake news actually referred to Russian propaganda and click bait, but Trump took it to mean news stories that one should not believe. This was perhaps the most important thing that he did during the presidential transition period. Trump did a good job of turning fake news into a slur, and this fit perfectly into Trump's campaign of disbelief. This is best represented by his statement in 2018 where he said that what people were seeing and reading were different from what was actually happening. He regularly, and disturbingly suggested that everything could be a hoax.

The rock of Fox's business model in 1996 was majorly disdain of, and disbelief of the news media. This also became the pillar of Trump's presidency. However, the anti-media stance was a part of even something bigger- the transformation of the Fox-fueled Republican Party. All that characterized the party pointed only to one thing- the rejection of expertise and resentment of anyone who claims to know better. This dominance of the Fox News had severe political implications which are only gaining ground now. One can call it brainwashing, as several conservatives currently refuse to even listen to any news or opinion not vetted through Fox, believing whatever appears on Fox as the gospel truth.

This however had terrible consequences during the coronavirus outbreak in 2020. At that time, Bartlett opined that Murdoch and the Fox brainwashing drama were risks to the health of the public. At this time, the president had been telling people to suspend belief for three full years. The very first time he did this was when he was in a rage against the U.S. intelligence community's conclusion that Russia intervened to help him win the election. Obama ordered a complete review of the Russian plot, Trump remained in denial about it. He told Chris Wallace of Fox News that it was just another excuse and that he did not believe it.

When he was put under pressure from the corps, he finally said he accepted the intel agencies' consensus view that Russia that was behind the cyberattack. Afterwards, CNN's exclusive about the Steele dossier was aired. The news story mentioned that Intel chiefs presented Trump with claims of Russian effort to compromise him. The story was fully packed, with the meeting described as it happened. Trump was shaken to his core, and a few hours later, he tweeted about fake news, referring to the news story as a total, political witch hunt.

The dossier was thirty-five pages filled with allegations of Trump's links to Russia. It was on everyone's lips. CNN did not publish the dossier's contents, since the info was not vetted and some of it was virtually impossible to confirm, but BuzzFeed went ahead to publish it, including the part about Trump supposedly paying Russian prostitutes for a golden showers show at the Ritz-Carlton in Moscow in 2013. BuzzFeed's stance was that the dossier's claims had already spread at the highest levels of the US government, and Americans should be able to read it and make their own decisions. Anchors at CNN were critical of BuzzFeed's decision, but it did not matter to Trump in the least. Instead, he attacked both media outlets and acted as though CNN printed the said claims. Using his press conference, he praised other media outlets while claiming to differentiate between good and bad media.

Some of the people who worked at the Fox saw through Trump's act. In response, Shep Smith said at the end of his show that although the Fox News could not confirm CNN's report, its correspondents followed journalistic standards and that neither they nor any other journalists should be subjected to belittling and delegitimizing by the president-elect of the United States. Shep claimed to be speaking on behalf of Fox News, but the truth remains that he could not truly speak for the entire network. In fact, Hannity did feel a thrill go up his leg while Trump spoke.

Trump and Hannity worked as a team to label the entire American news media as fake. The hypnotic message that both of them tried to pass was that Fox was the only legit network, and that the rest were fraudulent. On every episode of his show, Hannity made a point of note to reinforce this. Every night, he aired a collection of videos from commentators saying thigs he didn't like, cherry-picked information and a host of others. Hannity took examples of individual journalists acting friendly with the Clinton campaign, ignored the fact that the same coziness happened on the Trump side too, and alleged that all these major news organizations were colluding with Hillary. This nonsense, which he repeated every night was just propaganda to service Trump's campaign of disbelief.

THE CULT

KEY TAKEAWAYS

- The MAGAsphere particularly targeted journalists who revealed Trump's inconsistencies and falsehoods.
- Paul told Cavuto that the president would never talk to him, knowing that his news was fake.
- About one year into the Trump presidency administration, both his speeches and interviews lost whatever it was that made them generate huge ratings.
- Shep was the most known gay anchor at Fox News- a network with a terrible history of antigay commentary.

The emails trooped in, non-stop. Likewise the tweets. All of them were reflective of a well-coordinated campaign. As the Trump time went on, they intensified. The MAGAsphere particularly targeted journalists who revealed Trump's inconsistencies and falsehoods. Those who told the truth among Fox News workers were faced with some serious attacks as they were viewed as betrayers. Insiders from Fox said the hate emails became nastier as Trump's public loyalty demands became more and more extreme. Some of the news anchors made attempts to filter it out, but not Neil Cavuto. He went ahead and read the emails on air. Bold!

Cavuto did not hold Trump is such high regard. Neither did he think highly of Hannity. He believed that all Trump was getting from the prime-time players were bad advice, and therefore decided to use his 4pm show to need for restraint. He tried to dissuade Trump from going to war with Senate Republicans. He told Trump not to tweet tacky insults to critics, or scapegoat reporters. One afternoon, he told the president that it wasn't the fake news media that was his problem, but that he was by himself his own problem.

The suggestions weren't taken lightly. In fact, Paul told Cavuto that the president would never talk to him, knowing that his news was fake. Cavuto replied saying that he had never requested for a sit down with the president, saying that he did not think much would come out of it. What Hannity would never admit in public, Cavuto did- a ton of what Trump said in interviews was either uniformed, or outrightly untrue.

Trump was quite skilled at lying. He would look you squarely, in the eyes and lie to you, and he wouldn't even think he was lying, like Kellyanne Conway said in 2017. I once said it was scandalous that the president was lying about things like voter fraud and wiretapping, and Conway replied saying Trump doesn't think he's lying about those issues.

Another tendency Trump had was to contradict himself. This degraded the value of interviews with him, and Conway. Somehow, however, most of Fox News staff held on to the notion that presidential interviews had something newsworthy to them. Cavuto was an outlier by opting out. Fox's intramural competition to book Trump was fierce: Various friends slipped ratings reports to the president, sometimes verbally by phone, other times more formally by faxing and emailing printouts to various aides. Hannity, for example, wanted Trump to know that his show was much higher rated than Bret Baier's show, so that Trump didn't stray. Some of this ratings chatter was also about boosting Trump's ego. In his mind, if Fox was doing well, it meant he was doing well. He interpreted Fox's popularity as evidence of his own popularity.

About one year into the Trump presidency administration, both his speeches and interviews lost whatever it was that made them generate huge ratings. He became a regular caller on shows. If an interview made the news, it was simply because Trump felt pretty comfortable with the hosts that he must've said something rather inappropriate. His aides tried to intervene and stop these chats from happening, but they felt they could only tell him no so many times in a row.

Back in June 2013, Shep struck his first fifteen-million-dollar deal. Roger Ailes was still cutting the paychecks. The spectacular raise was a succor when Shep lost his 7 p.m. show. Ailes called all his stars into his conference room to talk about the new schedule.

Greta and Hannity were both about to move time slots in order to make way for Megyn Kelly at 9. Here, Shep was the odd host out. This decision reflected Ailes's view that the audience wanted red meat at dinnertime and not straight news. Basically, Shep was getting paid more to do less. How interesting.

Ailes also hurled ten million dollars at a new studio solely for Shep. He dubbed the Fox News Deck with walls of screens for the anchor and oversized iPads for the producers. This new place was where Shep would continue to anchor his 3 p.m. hour. His name had now been added to the title- Shepard Smith Reporting. This was also where he would anchor breaking news cut-ins during other people's shows. The entire thing was an effort to appease him and make the demotion appear as though it was a promotion.

However, everyone around the conference room table knew what it really was. One person present in the room at the time recalled that they knew right then that this was never going to work. Once in a while though, it worked, especially when mass shootings and other horrors required hours of rolling live coverage.

Ailes's other popular anchors however fought the Fox News Deck style. They insisted that they could handle any breaking news by themselves. For these people, TV airtime was like water. It had become necessary for survival. The TV executives began marking territories. This took a huge toll on the system, changing everything. It was clear that the rest of the network did not want him, and he wasted no time in relaxing into his happy life, off camera.

Shep was done with dating in 2012 when he settled down with Giovanni Graziano. Giovani was a production assistant on Shep's team. In order to avoid the obvious conflict, Giovani was transferred to a job at Fox Business. When Gawker revealed the relationship and outed Shep in 2013, Giovani was completely gone from the company.

Shep was completely gay. He was the most known gay anchor at Fox News- a network with a terrible history of antigay commentary. He once said he did not see the need to out himself, because he had never considered himself in. His co-workers and neighbors were fully aware that he was gay. However, his viewers were not. He began talking publicly about being gay in 2016, when he denied a Gawker report that claimed Ailes tried to keep Shep in the closet. Sometime in 2017, he mentioned to a group of college students that he goes to work, manages a lot of people, covers the news, deals with whatever is going on around him, and then goes home to the man he loves. He also said he goes home to family.

Reporting the truth about Trump put Shep at odds with Hannity and the others who, Shep said, were there strictly to be entertaining. He talked about the opinion-slingers in ways that were deeply insulting to them. Shep's jabs at prime time caused a stir, just like he intended.

THE CONTROL FREAK

KEY TAKEAWAYS

- Fox's shows were preoccupied with the emergence of AOC, alias Alexandria Ocasio-Cortez, who represented parts of both Queens and the Bronx.
- According to a research carried out in March, most Republicans had heard quite a lot about the Green New Deal.
- On the 4th of March, Mayer dropped a bomb in The New Yorker magazine.
- When Carlson claimed white supremacy was really not a real problem in America, Elleithee tweeted that the only set of people who believed that white supremacy was no real problem were white supremacists.

When the Democrats took over the White House following the 2018 midterm elections, it was a win for Fox as well. This was because the network remained most comfortable as the opposition. Fox's shows were preoccupied with the emergence of AOC, alias Alexandria Ocasio-Cortez, who represented parts of both Queens and the Bronx.

The attention-causing, twenty-nine-year-old congresswoman in addition to her promotion of a Green New Deal were like favors from the right-wing news gods. Within the first few weeks of the new term, Fox turned her into an object of hate, sowing fear of the climate change legislation.

According to a research carried out in March, most Republicans had heard quite a lot about the Green

New Deal. Those who heard of it hated it. Most Democrats heard very little about it. They however wanted to know more. The Fox effect had kicked in. This Fox effect was also called asymmetrical intensity. It suggests a situation when there's much more intense passion on one side than the other.

I asked AOC how she was coping with the passion on the right. I wanted to know if she was debating whether to appear on Fox and take her attackers head-on? She said she was. The same was the case with other Democrats. Very actively, the network was courting them for a very specific reason: to excite the advertisers who detested the bad press that came from the white identity politics of prime time. This was the very reason why Jane Mayer's timing was so detrimental to Fox.

On the 4th of March, Mayer dropped a bomb in The New Yorker magazine. Her undaunted look at Fox and the Murdochs gave protuberant Democrats a fresh motive to demand that Fox be omitted from the primary debate process. Honestly, I was surprised that Fox was even in contention, at all. Fox hadn't held an actual Democratic primary debate since 2004, and the channel had moved far to the right since then. Regardless, Jay Wallace was stern about securing a debate in the 2020 campaign season. Martha MacCallum and Bret Baier put him under pressure to make it happen. Wallace continually insisted that there were clear divisions between the two sides at Fox, even though most viewers could see that those partitions were melting away owing to ratings pressures and the audience's demands.

Anchors at Fox during the Bush years stated that things were never this prevalent. Anchors who counterattacked the pressures said they could notice the rightward bent nearly every sixty minutes. Bill Hemmer and Sandra Smith presented the late morning hours of America's Newsroom a more conservative edge than it had before. Trump was treated with kid gloves by Harris Faulkner on Outnumbered at noon. Baier's 6 p.m. Special Report panel became two on one, with two right-wing guests and a lone dissenter who was often a straitlaced news reporter. The bookings kept the programming on Trump's side. Shows like MacCallum's were referred to as hybrids or borderline shows because Fox counted them as news, but tin all honesty, they looked and sounded like opinion. By and large, viewers cared next to nothing about these nuances. All they wanted was to hear about their president. However, it mattered both internally and externally because Fox wanted to be seen as an influential media brand, not an arm for propaganda. Mayer's article dented all of that.

DNC chair, Tom Perez yielded to pressure from the left and banned Fox from the debate process, publicly. He cited the recent reporting in The New Yorker on the inappropriate relationship between President Trump, his administration and Fox News. Mayer only pointed out what Fox's viewers already knew and liked about the network, but the article pushed Democrats to ask once again if Fox were a legitimate news operation or majorly a political opponent.

A number of Democratic candidates swore off appearances on the channel. However, other

Democrats maintained that without being on Fox, you don't even have a chance of persuading Fox's America. Ex DNC spokesman, Mo Elleithee believed this very strongly. In fact, he went on to sign a contract with Fox back in 2016 based on this opinion. The whole thing appeared a flip-flop of the sort. This is because when he was running Comms at the party, he believed Democrats should shun the network, but when he left the committee in 2015, he began to see things in a whole, different light.

Elleithee loved to tell a story about the day a burly biker dude made a beeline for him. It was a holiday weekend in 2018 at the Dutch Wonderland amusement park in central Pennsylvania. The man stopped Elleithee's family as they were walking in between rides, asking if he was the Democratic dude on Fox, or not. Elleithee's wife was scared, and put her arm around their two kids. She took a step back, fearing the worst. Afterwards, the viewer said that Elleithee wrong most of the time, but he still appreciated what he had to say. The lesson therein was simple- Democrats needed to do a better job of listening and talking. Fox is one way to get that done. Still, he harbored reservations. Like many other Democrats, he hated Lou Dobbs' xenophobic segments and Carlson's white nationalist dog-whistling. When Carlson claimed white supremacy was really not a real problem in America, Elleithee tweeted that the only set of people who believed that white supremacy was no real problem were white supremacists.

On Friday, March 8, Shine resigned from his post. As usual, there was the normal hand-wringing about the implication of the communications director leaving, but really, it didn't mean a thing. Shine's absence wasn't really felt at the White House. In the absence of a daily briefing to study for, Sarah Huckabee Sanders had time to handle the responsibilities that fell to Shine. Later in the course of the year, Sanders left the White House, landing a higher-paying gig with Fox. Her replacement, Stephanie Grisham, never held a briefing and nearly completely gave TV interviews to Fox and other right-wing outlets like Sinclair. She intentionally went to the Fox bureau across town for most of her hits instead of standing at Fox's live shot location on the North Lawn like Kellyanne Conway did. Reporters at the White House concluded that Grisham was going out of her way to avoid being questioned by them after her Fox appearances. Again, it gave Fox another advantage. Grisham and Sanders confessed themselves that they would recommence briefings if Trump said so. All of these shots were called by him, and the Comms staff simply had to keep up. The result was dysfunction.

Fox's Steve Hilton found out that his long awaited request to interview Trump was being granted with just one day's advance notice. He took the next available flight and flew from L.A. to DC. Hilton was friend of Rupert's and a former adviser to British Prime Minister, David Cameron. Hilton hosted Fox's Sunday night show known as The Next Revolution. On the show, he promoted something he called positive populism, and became more optimistic about Trump as the years rolled by. He considered Trump's words wrong but his actions, right. The more praise Hilton gave those actions on air, the more Trump watched on Sunday nights. This led to this rather abrupt interview.

The White House press shop told Hilton that he would only get fifteen minutes with the president. However, Trump was in a chatty mood and went on for forty-five minutes. Hilton tried to end the interview, scared of what Trump's aides might do to him. Trump assured him nothing would happen. According to data collected by presidential historian, Martha Kumar, the Hilton sit-down was Trump's sixty-fifth interview with Fox. Every fortnight, he had a chat with Fox. As for other national TV stations, interviews were few and far between. Trump was clearly not trying to appeal to CNN or ABC viewers. Rather, he just wanted to keep Fox viewers satiated.

Sadly, as Shine's underwhelming performance at the White House showed, the Fox obsession kept backfiring on Trump.

THE CRISIS

KEY TAKEAWAYS

- In her testimony, Hill made some of the most troubling evidence of Fox's influence on the highest levels of government common knowledge.
- When Fox's polling unit held that 50 percent of Americans wanted Trump impeached and removed, Hannity disregarded the data completely.
- Hannity's response to the third impeachment vote by the House of Representatives in American history was pre-taped at his home on Long Island. That night, right along with 5 million other people, I was duped.
- On February 5, 2020, Republicans in the Senate acquitted the president on both the abuse of power and obstruction counts.

Dr. Fiona Hill said that in the Trump White House, the television was always on. In addition, it was usually on Fox News. She was once Trump's most senior adviser on European and Russian affairs. If anyone understood things, she knew it was a risky position to hold. However, she never expected that she'd one day be a star witness at an impeachment inquiry. In her testimony, Hill made some of the most troubling evidence of Fox's influence on the highest levels of government common knowledge. She mentioned that the tumultuous Ukraine disinformation that spewed from Rudy, John Solomon, and other Fox regulars made her job nearly impossible to perform.

Whenever Hill met with John Bolton in his office, and Rudy was live on Fox, Bolton turned up the volume to hear what he was saying. Hill discovered that significant parts of the pressure campaign played out right on TV for everyone to see. A massive mountain of evidence showed that the blame-Ukraine scheme was sown, and supported by, Fox. Sadly, the president failed to rethink the value of those friendships.

The more his gross misconduct regarding Ukraine was exposed in October and November, Trump needed Fox more than ever. Hannity became full of defenses, knocking down the total sham Schiff show charade every night. When Fox's polling unit held that 50 percent of Americans wanted Trump impeached and removed, Hannity disregarded the data completely. Other shows also played their parts. For instance, Fox & Friends producers wrote wackadoo talking points like *media declares trump should be impeached*, as though the media were a single person, Ingraham attacked the Dems night after night, and Carlson made jest of other news outlets for taking the scandal with so much seriousness.

As a result of these actions, the House impeachment inquiry stretched in two totally different news worlds. Weeks of unfavorable testimony were jammed by weeks of insults hailed directly at the witnesses. Fox's biggest stars tried to delegitimize the process and demonize the Dems. Hannity continued to claim that Ukraine interfered in 2016, thereby creating a totally fake correspondence between Russia's multi-pronged attack and the sloppy actions of some individual Ukrainians. These lies worked in the world outside DC.

A polling found that Fox viewers were more likely to say Ukraine interfered and less likely to say Russia interfered, when compared against people who largely watched other channels. Democratic lawmakers pointed out that the president's reliance on this alternative reality was part of the problem. Senate Minority Leader, Chuck Schumer rebuked Trump for buying into baseless conspiracy theories told by known liars on Fox News. Ironically, Schumer's office also bragged about the number of Democrats who went on Fox to perforate the bubble and present evidence of high crimes and misdemeanors.

The final vote on two articles of impeachment was slated for prime time- Wednesday, December 18. Hannity had other plans. He knew that Trump, along with millions of his fans would be glued to his 9 p.m. monologue, desperately seeking for assurance that the impeachment was nothing but a lie, a sham, a hoax. That same night, he also knew he had a family obligation. Hence, Hannity's response to the third impeachment vote by the House of Representatives in American history was pre-taped at his home on Long Island. That night, right along with 5 million other people, I was duped.

I sincerely thought he was live, like every other host was, on every other channel. This was the most important news day of the year. How could he not be? Reason was because no one in charge at Fox had the audacity to tell him no. Hannity's producers did everything they could to mask the fact that the show was stale. People on the other side of the Fox fence were irritated by Hannity's lazy behavior. When people found out Sean taped his show, they flipped. Bret Baier was particularly angry. Like his colleague on other networks, he could have been anchoring the network's live coverage. As a matter of fact, in the past, he would have been in the anchor chair. But Trump had transformed Fox. Now, the network valued the attention of Trump's America the most, regardless of news, facts and traditions. Whether it was embarrassing or not, no one in Fox management really thought straight-edged news coverage would have out-rated Hannity's outdated charade. And that's what mattered most: The Scoreboard.

Besides climactic moments like December 18, Baier kept his cool. Everyone in his social circle said that he was the sensible one left at Fox. At a glittery party for Baier's new book in DC in the fall, an attendee remarked thanking God for Bret and Chris Wallace. A friend of Bret's also mentioned to me that she was shocked to see a CNN anchor at a Fox anchor's party. She reckoned the atmosphere had become too toxic to allow for such a thing. Truth be told, it almost had.

In history, these ingratiating kinds of events were the media form of bipartisanship. Sure enough, at Baier's party, I spotted Jonathan Karl from ABC, Norah O'Donnell from CBS and Mike Allen from Axios. Nonetheless, the venom was real. Some of Baier's friendships weakened in the Trump years. Journalists at other networks said they were disappointed by his two-sided type of coverage in an era where one side lied so much more than the other side.

Since impeachment became hung as a remedy to check Trump's misconduct in 2017, historians and experts had brought up the Fox factor. Often times, it came up hypothetically. If Richard Nixon had had Fox and an entire universe of right-wing media, would he have been forced from office, or could he have hung on? In 2020, the answer was revealed. The Fox war room shifted from defense to offense for the Senate trial and the preordained ending to the impeachment saga. A slew of Fox regulars jumped from the studio to the Senate chamber to take up Trump's cause. Ken Starr, whose work as an independent counsel eventually led to the impeachment of Bill Clinton and who became a paid Fox News contributor in 2019 when management anticipated another impeachment drama, took a leave from the network to join Trump's defense team. Frequent Fox guests Alan Dershowitz, Pam Bondi, Jay Sekulow, and Robert Ray all joined as well. When Ray got the gig, he thanked Maria Bartiromo for putting him on TV. He was right. Fox's defense team put on a show for Fox's airwaves. Hannity picked up where they left off in the evening and he pressured wayward Republican senators to stay in line. He addressed perceived swing voters Susan Collins and Mitt Romney directly through the camera, threatening that their voters would not tolerate any dissent. Everyone got the message: No new witnesses. No new evidence. Let Trump get back to work.

Maureen Dowd summed up the strategy perfectly when she said the Democrats are relying on facts, but the Republicans are relying on Fox. On February 5, 2020, Republicans in the Senate acquitted the president on both the abuse of power and obstruction counts. Democratic senator, Sherrod Brown told me he saw fear in the eyes of his Republican counterparts. He said it was the fear of Fox, the fear of talk radio. And most of all it was fear of the president, who took his cues from those sources.

EPILOGUE

KEY TAKEAWAYS

- Fox wingmen encouraged Trump to do like a cable news bomb-thrower: to pick fights instead of finding common ground, to govern for TV ratings instead of tangible results, to supply endless content for talk shows.
- Trump told Sean Hannity that the virus was fading away, even as U.S. cases surged and the death toll climbed well above one hundred thousand.
- America was going through a reckoning and that it was unclear where the country's most watched cable channel, and possibly one of the most powerful political establishments in American history will come out of that reckoning.
- Another election looms.
- Trusting in the Fox News president was the biggest hoax of all.

Being ruled by a Fox News president left the rest of the country without a properly functioning chief executive from 2017 until 2020. At the beginning of 2017, Trump needed help. He needed scrutinized information. He desired to hear the truth from people he respected. He also needed to be held accountable. Rather than be provided with those, many Fox wingmen fed his worst impulses and helped him deceive the very people who voted him into power. They encouraged him to do like a cable news bomb-thrower: to pick fights instead of finding common ground, to govern for TV ratings instead of tangible results, to supply endless content for talk shows. And, in 2020, to fuel denialism about the coronavirus pandemic.

Trump spoke about the coronavirus in the past tense. He told Sean Hannity that the virus was fading away, even as U.S. cases surged and the death toll climbed well above one hundred thousand. Trump resumed public events and refused to wear a mask in public in disobedience to his own government's recommendations. He also contradicted what Fox was doing. At Fox News Head Quarters in late June, staffers who weren't able to work from home were reminded to wear a mask whenever they were in shared office spaces. Again, and again, the company's plans for a fuller return to work were postponed due to safety concerns. Fox's anchors knew all of this but rarely challenged Trump's irresponsible and ignorant conduct on the air. Profits over principle: That was the significance of the Trump ages.

Throughout the Trump presidency, there were straight lines from Fox's misguided segments to Trump's mistakes. Those who tried to correct him, e.g., Shep Smith, Neil Cavuto and Chris Wallace, were maligned. Those who excused his misconduct were idolized. In the summer of 2020, there were no signs that this would change at Fox. The country was however changing fast. When protests over the murder of George Floyd erupted in Minneapolis in late May, Fox's programming was uneven. The country felt like a powder keg, with lopsided illness and fatalities from Covid-19 among black, brown, and poor people. This was in addition to massive unemployment and viral videos of police brutality totaling an unparalleled nationwide protest effort. Support for the Black Lives Matter movement was at record highs.

Fox's law and order programming felt out of step amidst a national dialogue about how law enforcement was failing so many Americans. A Fox commentator told me that America was going through a reckoning and that it was unclear where the country's most watched cable channel, and possibly one of the most powerful political establishments in American history will come out of that reckoning.

Another election looms. Barack Obama said in April 2020 when he endorsed Joe Biden for president that the future of America hangs on this election, and that it won't be easy. Obama viewed Trump and Fox as the zenith of decades of Republican Party trend lines. While Fox held the GOP's shrinking coalition together, polls showed that it wouldn't be enough to win Trump a second term. Hannity tried out different anti-Biden talking points every night, and said America would be unrecognizable if Trump lost, but the host seemed tired of his own hyperbole.

Tucker Carlson, always the savvier operator, looked beyond 2020. His monologues sounded like post-Trump presidential stump speeches. Several of his colleagues told me they could see Carlson on the primary ballot in 2024. The Trump age was really the hoax age. Fox viewers came away with the impression that nothing was truly knowable. Everything was relative. There were distortions and deceptions in every direction. Up could be down and left could be right and real news could be fake. Many people, exhausted by the uncertainty, gave up on knowing for sure whether Russia had helped Trump win the 2016 election, or if the administration was doing all it could to end the pandemic.

Hoax was uttered more than nine hundred times on Fox News in the first six months of 2020. Every time Trump tweeted it, or Hannity shouted it, a little bit more truth was chipped away from America's foundation, exactly at a time when the country was beset by multiple crises and needed honesty and accuracy, compassion and sound science. The lying extended predictably to social media smears about anti-racism protesters, lies that both echoed and foreshadowed lines of attack and denial by Fox personalities.

White House officials lied when they denied having used tear gas to clear a path through a nonthreatening crowd in Lafayette Park for a presidential photo op. Trump lied about crowd size when the streets swelled with peaceful protesters, whom he linked to terrorists and anarchists. Having no truth to tell the public, ever, he set the people against each other, stirring up strife. He told the public not to believe their own eyes and ears, and he thought he could get away with it because, on Fox, arguably his only reality, he always did. Just trust in the Fox News president. That was the biggest hoax of all.